50 Kids Lunchbox Recipes

By: Kelly Johnson

Table of Contents

- Mini Turkey and Cheese Sandwiches
- Veggie Quesadillas
- Chicken Caesar Wraps
- Hummus and Veggie Sticks
- Cheese and Crackers
- Pita Pockets with Chicken Salad
- Fruit and Nut Butter Wraps
- Mini Meatballs with Marinara Sauce
- Turkey and Avocado Pinwheels
- Veggie and Cheese Skewers
- Peanut Butter and Banana Sandwiches
- Chicken and Veggie Skewers
- Apple Slices with Yogurt Dip
- Homemade Lunchables with Ham, Cheese, and Crackers
- Chicken Nuggets with Carrot Sticks
- Macaroni and Cheese Muffins
- Veggie Hummus Wraps
- Rice Cakes with Cream Cheese and Cucumber
- Mini Bagel Pizzas
- Whole Grain Muffins
- Rice Paper Rolls with Veggies and Tofu
- Hard-Boiled Eggs with Veggie Sticks
- Pita Chips with Guacamole
- Turkey and Cheese Roll-Ups
- Apple and Almond Butter Sandwiches
- Greek Yogurt with Honey and Berries
- DIY Taco Cups
- Avocado Toast with Cherry Tomatoes
- Pizza Stuffed Rolls
- Tuna Salad with Crackers
- Sweet Potato Fries with Ketchup
- Veggie-Stuffed Pita
- Chicken and Spinach Pinwheels
- Cucumber and Cream Cheese Sandwiches
- Fruit Kabobs with Yogurt Dip

- Spinach and Cheese Stuffed Muffins
- Grilled Cheese and Tomato Soup Cups
- Mini Pancake Skewers with Fruit
- Veggie Frittata Bites
- Banana Oatmeal Cookies
- Chicken Salad Lettuce Cups
- Pita Bread Pizza
- Cucumber, Carrot, and Hummus Wraps
- Mini Cornbread Muffins
- Cheesy Broccoli and Rice Cups
- Fruit and Cheese Kabobs
- Homemade Granola Bars
- Veggie and Cheese Empanadas
- Chicken and Rice Salad
- Apple and Cheddar Cheese Slices

Mini Turkey and Cheese Sandwiches

Ingredients:

- 12 mini sandwich rolls or slider buns
- 12 slices deli turkey
- 12 slices cheese (Swiss, cheddar, or your choice)
- 1 tablespoon Dijon mustard (optional)
- 1 tablespoon mayonnaise (optional)
- Lettuce leaves (optional)

Instructions:

1. Slice the mini rolls in half and spread a little Dijon mustard or mayonnaise on the inside (if desired).
2. Layer a slice of cheese and a slice of turkey on the bottom half of each roll.
3. Top with a lettuce leaf if desired, then place the top half of the roll on each sandwich.
4. Serve immediately or refrigerate for later.

Veggie Quesadillas

Ingredients:

- 4 flour tortillas
- 1 cup shredded cheese (cheddar, mozzarella, or a blend)
- 1 cup bell peppers, diced
- 1/2 cup onions, diced
- 1/2 cup corn kernels (fresh or frozen)
- 1/2 cup black beans, drained and rinsed
- 1 tablespoon olive oil
- Salt and pepper to taste
- Sour cream or salsa for dipping

Instructions:

1. Heat olive oil in a skillet over medium heat. Sauté bell peppers, onions, corn, and black beans for 3-5 minutes until tender. Season with salt and pepper.
2. Heat a separate pan over medium-low heat. Place a tortilla in the pan, sprinkle with cheese, and top with the veggie mixture.
3. Place a second tortilla on top, and cook for 2-3 minutes per side, until golden brown and the cheese has melted.
4. Slice into wedges and serve with sour cream or salsa.

Chicken Caesar Wraps

Ingredients:

- 2 cooked chicken breasts, sliced
- 4 large flour tortillas
- 1/2 cup Caesar dressing
- 1 cup Romaine lettuce, chopped
- 1/2 cup grated Parmesan cheese
- Croutons (optional)

Instructions:

1. In a bowl, toss the sliced chicken with Caesar dressing until evenly coated.
2. Lay the tortillas flat and place a handful of chopped lettuce in the center.
3. Add the dressed chicken, Parmesan cheese, and croutons.
4. Roll up the tortilla tightly, folding in the sides as you go.
5. Slice in half and serve.

Hummus and Veggie Sticks

Ingredients:

- 1 cup hummus (store-bought or homemade)
- Assorted veggie sticks: carrots, cucumbers, celery, bell peppers, etc.

Instructions:

1. Arrange the veggie sticks on a serving plate.
2. Serve with a bowl of hummus for dipping.

Cheese and Crackers

Ingredients:

- Assorted cheese (cheddar, brie, gouda, etc.)
- Crackers (Ritz, water crackers, or your choice)

Instructions:

1. Slice the cheese into small wedges or cubes.
2. Arrange the cheese and crackers on a serving platter.
3. Serve as an easy, elegant appetizer or snack.

Pita Pockets with Chicken Salad

Ingredients:

- 4 pita pockets
- 2 cups cooked chicken breast, shredded
- 1/2 cup mayonnaise or Greek yogurt
- 1 tablespoon Dijon mustard
- 1/4 cup diced celery
- 1/4 cup diced red onion
- Salt and pepper to taste
- Lettuce leaves

Instructions:

1. In a bowl, mix the shredded chicken, mayonnaise (or yogurt), Dijon mustard, celery, red onion, salt, and pepper.
2. Slice the pita pockets in half and stuff with lettuce leaves and the chicken salad mixture.
3. Serve immediately or chill for later.

Fruit and Nut Butter Wraps

Ingredients:

- 4 whole wheat tortillas
- 1/2 cup almond or peanut butter
- 1 banana, sliced
- 1/2 cup mixed berries (strawberries, blueberries, etc.)
- Honey (optional)

Instructions:

1. Spread a thin layer of almond or peanut butter on each tortilla.
2. Add slices of banana and mixed berries on top.
3. Drizzle with honey (if desired), then roll up the tortilla tightly.
4. Slice into pinwheels and serve.

Mini Meatballs with Marinara Sauce

Ingredients:

- 1 lb ground beef or turkey
- 1/2 cup breadcrumbs
- 1 egg
- 1/4 cup grated Parmesan cheese
- 1 teaspoon garlic powder
- 1 teaspoon dried oregano
- Salt and pepper to taste
- 1 cup marinara sauce

Instructions:

1. Preheat the oven to 375°F (190°C).
2. In a bowl, mix the ground meat, breadcrumbs, egg, Parmesan, garlic powder, oregano, salt, and pepper.
3. Roll the mixture into small meatballs, about 1 inch in diameter, and place them on a baking sheet.
4. Bake for 15-20 minutes, or until cooked through.
5. Heat the marinara sauce in a saucepan and serve with the meatballs for dipping.

Turkey and Avocado Pinwheels

Ingredients:

- 4 large flour tortillas
- 8 slices deli turkey
- 1 ripe avocado, mashed
- 1/4 cup cream cheese
- 1 cup spinach or lettuce
- 1 tablespoon Dijon mustard (optional)

Instructions:

1. Spread a thin layer of cream cheese and mashed avocado onto each tortilla.
2. Place two slices of turkey and a handful of spinach or lettuce on top.
3. Roll the tortilla tightly and slice into pinwheels.
4. Serve immediately or wrap and refrigerate for later.

Veggie and Cheese Skewers

Ingredients:

- 1 cup cherry tomatoes
- 1 cucumber, sliced into rounds
- 1 bell pepper, cut into chunks
- 1 small zucchini, sliced
- 1 cup cheese cubes (cheddar, mozzarella, or your choice)
- Olive oil, salt, and pepper for drizzling

Instructions:

1. On wooden skewers, alternate threading the veggies and cheese cubes.
2. Drizzle with olive oil and sprinkle with salt and pepper.
3. Grill or bake at 375°F (190°C) for 10-15 minutes until veggies are slightly tender.
4. Serve immediately.

Peanut Butter and Banana Sandwiches

Ingredients:

- 2 slices whole grain or white bread
- 2 tablespoons peanut butter
- 1 banana, sliced

Instructions:

1. Spread peanut butter on one side of each slice of bread.
2. Layer the banana slices on one slice of bread.
3. Close the sandwich and slice into halves or quarters.
4. Serve immediately.

Chicken and Veggie Skewers

Ingredients:

- 2 chicken breasts, cubed
- 1 bell pepper, cut into chunks
- 1 onion, cut into chunks
- 1 zucchini, sliced
- 1 tablespoon olive oil
- Salt and pepper to taste
- 1 teaspoon dried oregano or Italian seasoning

Instructions:

1. Preheat grill or grill pan to medium heat.
2. Thread the chicken and veggies onto skewers.
3. Drizzle with olive oil and season with salt, pepper, and oregano.
4. Grill for 10-15 minutes, turning occasionally, until chicken is fully cooked.
5. Serve hot.

Apple Slices with Yogurt Dip

Ingredients:

- 2 apples, sliced
- 1/2 cup plain Greek yogurt
- 1 tablespoon honey
- 1/2 teaspoon cinnamon

Instructions:

1. Slice the apples into wedges.
2. In a small bowl, mix the yogurt with honey and cinnamon.
3. Serve the apple slices with the yogurt dip.

Homemade Lunchables with Ham, Cheese, and Crackers

Ingredients:

- 4 slices deli ham
- 4 slices cheese (cheddar, mozzarella, or your choice)
- 1 cup crackers (Ritz or your favorite variety)
- 1/4 cup baby carrots (optional)
- 1/4 cup cucumber slices (optional)

Instructions:

1. Arrange the ham slices, cheese slices, and crackers in small compartments of a lunchbox.
2. Add optional veggies like baby carrots and cucumber slices.
3. Serve immediately or pack for later.

Chicken Nuggets with Carrot Sticks

Ingredients:

- 1 lb chicken breast, cut into bite-sized pieces
- 1 cup breadcrumbs
- 1/2 cup grated Parmesan cheese
- 1 egg, beaten
- Salt and pepper to taste
- 2 tablespoons olive oil
- 1 cup baby carrots, for serving

Instructions:

1. Preheat the oven to 400°F (200°C).
2. Dip chicken pieces in the beaten egg, then coat in breadcrumbs and Parmesan.
3. Place on a baking sheet, drizzle with olive oil, and bake for 15-20 minutes until golden brown.
4. Serve with carrot sticks for dipping.

Macaroni and Cheese Muffins

Ingredients:

- 2 cups cooked macaroni pasta
- 1 1/2 cups shredded cheese (cheddar or your choice)
- 1/2 cup milk
- 2 eggs, beaten
- 1/2 cup breadcrumbs
- Salt and pepper to taste

Instructions:

1. Preheat oven to 375°F (190°C) and grease a muffin tin.
2. In a bowl, mix the cooked pasta, cheese, milk, and beaten eggs. Season with salt and pepper.
3. Spoon the mixture into the muffin tin, filling each cup.
4. Top with breadcrumbs and bake for 15-20 minutes, until golden and firm.
5. Let cool slightly before serving.

Veggie Hummus Wraps

Ingredients:

- 4 whole wheat tortillas
- 1 cup hummus (store-bought or homemade)
- 1 cup shredded lettuce
- 1/2 cucumber, thinly sliced
- 1/2 bell pepper, thinly sliced
- 1/4 cup shredded carrots

Instructions:

1. Spread a generous amount of hummus on each tortilla.
2. Layer the veggies (lettuce, cucumber, bell pepper, carrots) on top.
3. Roll up the tortilla tightly and slice into pinwheels.
4. Serve immediately.

Rice Cakes with Cream Cheese and Cucumber

Ingredients:

- 4 plain rice cakes
- 1/4 cup cream cheese
- 1/2 cucumber, thinly sliced
- Salt and pepper to taste

Instructions:

1. Spread a thin layer of cream cheese on each rice cake.
2. Top with thin cucumber slices.
3. Season with a little salt and pepper.
4. Serve immediately or refrigerate for later.

Mini Bagel Pizzas

Ingredients:

- 4 mini bagels, halved
- 1/2 cup marinara sauce
- 1 cup shredded mozzarella cheese
- 1/4 cup pepperoni or your choice of toppings (mushrooms, olives, etc.)
- 1 teaspoon dried oregano

Instructions:

1. Preheat the oven to 375°F (190°C).
2. Spread marinara sauce on each bagel half.
3. Top with shredded mozzarella and your choice of toppings.
4. Sprinkle with dried oregano.
5. Place the bagels on a baking sheet and bake for 10-12 minutes, until cheese is melted and bubbly.
6. Serve immediately.

Whole Grain Muffins

Ingredients:

- 1 cup whole grain flour
- 1/2 cup rolled oats
- 1/2 cup honey or maple syrup
- 1/2 cup milk
- 1/4 cup vegetable oil
- 1 egg
- 1 teaspoon baking powder
- 1/2 teaspoon baking soda
- 1/2 teaspoon cinnamon
- 1/4 teaspoon salt

Instructions:

1. Preheat the oven to 350°F (175°C) and line a muffin tin with paper liners.
2. In a large bowl, whisk together the flour, oats, baking powder, baking soda, cinnamon, and salt.
3. In another bowl, combine the honey, milk, oil, and egg.
4. Add the wet ingredients to the dry ingredients and stir until just combined.
5. Spoon the batter into the muffin tin and bake for 18-20 minutes, until a toothpick comes out clean.
6. Let cool before serving.

Rice Paper Rolls with Veggies and Tofu

Ingredients:

- 6 rice paper sheets
- 1/2 block firm tofu, sliced into strips
- 1 cup shredded carrots
- 1/2 cucumber, thinly sliced
- 1/2 bell pepper, thinly sliced
- Fresh cilantro and mint leaves
- Soy sauce or peanut dipping sauce for serving

Instructions:

1. Soak the rice paper sheets in warm water for about 10 seconds, until soft.
2. Lay the rice paper on a clean surface and arrange tofu strips, carrots, cucumber, bell pepper, and herbs in the center.
3. Fold in the sides and roll up the rice paper tightly.
4. Repeat with the remaining ingredients.
5. Serve with soy sauce or peanut dipping sauce.

Hard-Boiled Eggs with Veggie Sticks

Ingredients:

- 4 large eggs
- 1 cup carrot sticks
- 1 cup cucumber sticks
- Salt and pepper to taste

Instructions:

1. Place eggs in a saucepan and cover with water. Bring to a boil.
2. Reduce heat and simmer for 10-12 minutes. Remove eggs from the water and let cool.
3. Peel the eggs and cut them into halves or quarters.
4. Serve with carrot and cucumber sticks on the side, seasoned with salt and pepper.

Pita Chips with Guacamole

Ingredients:

- 2 pita bread rounds
- 1 tablespoon olive oil
- Salt to taste
- 2 ripe avocados
- 1/4 cup red onion, finely chopped
- 1/2 lime, juiced
- 1 small tomato, chopped
- 1 teaspoon cilantro, chopped (optional)

Instructions:

1. Preheat the oven to 375°F (190°C).
2. Cut the pita bread into triangles and brush with olive oil.
3. Sprinkle with salt and bake for 8-10 minutes, until crispy.
4. For the guacamole, mash the avocados in a bowl and mix with red onion, lime juice, tomato, and cilantro.
5. Serve the pita chips with guacamole.

Turkey and Cheese Roll-Ups

Ingredients:

- 6 slices turkey breast
- 6 slices cheese (cheddar, mozzarella, or your choice)
- 1 tablespoon Dijon mustard or mayonnaise (optional)

Instructions:

1. Lay a slice of turkey on a flat surface.
2. Place a slice of cheese on top.
3. Roll up the turkey and cheese, securing with a toothpick if needed.
4. Serve immediately or pack for later.

Apple and Almond Butter Sandwiches

Ingredients:

- 2 apples, cored and sliced into rounds
- 2 tablespoons almond butter
- 1/4 teaspoon cinnamon (optional)

Instructions:

1. Spread almond butter on one apple slice.
2. Top with another apple slice to create a sandwich.
3. Sprinkle with cinnamon if desired.
4. Serve immediately.

Greek Yogurt with Honey and Berries

Ingredients:

- 1 cup plain Greek yogurt
- 1 tablespoon honey
- 1/2 cup mixed berries (blueberries, raspberries, strawberries)

Instructions:

1. Spoon the Greek yogurt into a bowl.
2. Drizzle with honey and top with fresh berries.
3. Serve immediately.

DIY Taco Cups

Ingredients:

- 6 small flour tortillas
- 1 lb ground beef or chicken, cooked
- 1/2 cup shredded cheese
- 1/4 cup salsa
- 1/4 cup sour cream
- 1/4 cup chopped lettuce
- 1/4 cup diced tomatoes

Instructions:

1. Preheat the oven to 375°F (190°C).
2. Cut the tortillas into small circles (use a cup or cookie cutter) and press them into a muffin tin to form small taco cups.
3. Bake the tortilla cups for 10 minutes until crispy.
4. Fill the cups with cooked ground meat, top with cheese, and return to the oven for 5 minutes to melt the cheese.
5. Serve with salsa, sour cream, lettuce, and tomatoes.

Avocado Toast with Cherry Tomatoes

Ingredients:

- 2 slices whole grain or sourdough bread
- 1 ripe avocado
- 1/2 cup cherry tomatoes, halved
- Salt and pepper to taste
- Olive oil drizzle (optional)

Instructions:

1. Toast the bread to your desired crispiness.
2. Mash the avocado and spread it on the toasted bread.
3. Top with halved cherry tomatoes and season with salt and pepper.
4. Drizzle with olive oil if desired.
5. Serve immediately.

Pizza Stuffed Rolls

Ingredients:

- 1 pizza dough (store-bought or homemade)
- 1/2 cup marinara sauce
- 1 cup shredded mozzarella cheese
- 1/4 cup pepperoni or other pizza toppings
- 1 tablespoon olive oil
- 1/2 teaspoon dried oregano

Instructions:

1. Preheat the oven to 375°F (190°C).
2. Roll out the pizza dough into a rectangle.
3. Spread marinara sauce over the dough, leaving a border.
4. Sprinkle with mozzarella cheese and your choice of toppings.
5. Roll up the dough tightly and cut into slices.
6. Place the rolls on a baking sheet and brush with olive oil.
7. Sprinkle with oregano and bake for 15-20 minutes until golden brown.
8. Serve with extra marinara sauce for dipping.

Tuna Salad with Crackers

Ingredients:

- 1 can tuna in water, drained
- 2 tablespoons mayonnaise
- 1 tablespoon Dijon mustard (optional)
- 1/4 cup diced celery
- 1/4 cup diced red onion
- Salt and pepper to taste
- Crackers for serving

Instructions:

1. In a bowl, combine the drained tuna, mayonnaise, mustard, celery, and red onion.
2. Mix well and season with salt and pepper.
3. Serve with crackers for dipping or spreading.

Sweet Potato Fries with Ketchup

Ingredients:

- 2 large sweet potatoes, peeled and cut into fries
- 1 tablespoon olive oil
- Salt and pepper to taste
- 1/2 teaspoon paprika (optional)
- Ketchup for dipping

Instructions:

1. Preheat the oven to 400°F (200°C).
2. Toss the sweet potato fries in olive oil, salt, pepper, and paprika.
3. Spread them out in a single layer on a baking sheet.
4. Bake for 25-30 minutes, flipping halfway through, until crispy and golden.
5. Serve with ketchup for dipping.

Veggie-Stuffed Pita

Ingredients:

- 4 pita pockets
- 1 cucumber, sliced
- 1 tomato, diced
- 1/4 red onion, thinly sliced
- 1/2 cup hummus
- 1/4 cup feta cheese (optional)
- Fresh parsley for garnish

Instructions:

1. Cut the pita pockets in half.
2. Spread a tablespoon of hummus inside each pita half.
3. Stuff the pita with cucumber, tomato, onion, and feta.
4. Garnish with fresh parsley and serve.

Chicken and Spinach Pinwheels

Ingredients:

- 2 large flour tortillas
- 1 cup cooked chicken breast, shredded
- 1/2 cup fresh spinach, chopped
- 1/4 cup cream cheese, softened
- 1 tablespoon Dijon mustard (optional)
- Salt and pepper to taste

Instructions:

1. Spread a thin layer of cream cheese on each tortilla.
2. Add shredded chicken and spinach on top.
3. Drizzle with Dijon mustard, if desired, and season with salt and pepper.
4. Roll up the tortillas tightly and slice into pinwheels.
5. Serve immediately or refrigerate for later.

Cucumber and Cream Cheese Sandwiches

Ingredients:

- 4 slices whole grain bread
- 4 tablespoons cream cheese
- 1/2 cucumber, thinly sliced
- Salt and pepper to taste
- Fresh dill for garnish (optional)

Instructions:

1. Spread cream cheese on each slice of bread.
2. Layer the cucumber slices on top of the cream cheese.
3. Sprinkle with salt and pepper.
4. Cut into small sandwiches or serve as open-faced sandwiches.
5. Garnish with fresh dill, if desired.

Fruit Kabobs with Yogurt Dip

Ingredients:

- 1 apple, chopped
- 1 banana, sliced
- 1 cup strawberries, hulled and halved
- 1/2 cup grapes, halved
- Wooden skewers
- 1/2 cup Greek yogurt
- 1 tablespoon honey
- 1/2 teaspoon vanilla extract

Instructions:

1. Thread the chopped fruit onto the wooden skewers.
2. In a small bowl, mix together the yogurt, honey, and vanilla extract to make the dip.
3. Serve the fruit kabobs with the yogurt dip on the side.

Spinach and Cheese Stuffed Muffins

Ingredients:

- 1 cup fresh spinach, chopped
- 1 cup shredded cheese (cheddar or mozzarella)
- 1 cup flour
- 1/2 cup milk
- 1/4 cup olive oil
- 1 egg
- 1 teaspoon baking powder
- Salt and pepper to taste

Instructions:

1. Preheat the oven to 350°F (175°C) and grease a muffin tin.
2. In a bowl, whisk together flour, baking powder, salt, and pepper.
3. In another bowl, whisk together the egg, milk, and olive oil.
4. Combine the wet and dry ingredients, then fold in the spinach and cheese.
5. Spoon the mixture into the muffin tin and bake for 15-20 minutes, until golden brown.
6. Let cool slightly before serving.

Grilled Cheese and Tomato Soup Cups

Ingredients:

- 4 slices of bread
- 4 slices of cheese (cheddar or American)
- 1 tablespoon butter
- 1 cup tomato soup
- 4 small cups for serving

Instructions:

1. Heat the tomato soup on the stove or microwave.
2. Butter one side of each slice of bread and place cheese between two slices, butter side out.
3. Grill the sandwich in a skillet over medium heat until both sides are golden brown and cheese is melted.
4. Slice the grilled cheese into small squares and serve in cups with tomato soup for dipping.

Mini Pancake Skewers with Fruit

Ingredients:

- 1 batch of mini pancakes (or store-bought)
- 1/2 cup strawberries, halved
- 1/2 banana, sliced
- 1/2 cup blueberries
- Wooden skewers
- Maple syrup for dipping

Instructions:

1. Cook mini pancakes and let them cool slightly.
2. Thread the pancakes and fruit onto the wooden skewers in alternating layers.
3. Serve with maple syrup for dipping.

Veggie Frittata Bites

Ingredients:

- 6 large eggs
- 1/2 cup milk
- 1/2 cup diced bell peppers
- 1/4 cup chopped spinach
- 1/4 cup shredded cheese
- Salt and pepper to taste

Instructions:

1. Preheat the oven to 350°F (175°C) and grease a mini muffin tin.
2. In a bowl, whisk the eggs and milk together. Add the bell peppers, spinach, cheese, salt, and pepper.
3. Pour the mixture into the muffin tin, filling each cup about 3/4 full.
4. Bake for 15-20 minutes, or until the frittata bites are set and golden brown.
5. Let cool slightly before serving.

Banana Oatmeal Cookies

Ingredients:

- 2 ripe bananas, mashed
- 1 cup rolled oats
- 1/2 cup raisins or chocolate chips (optional)
- 1/2 teaspoon cinnamon
- 1/4 teaspoon vanilla extract

Instructions:

1. Preheat the oven to 350°F (175°C) and line a baking sheet with parchment paper.
2. In a bowl, combine the mashed bananas, oats, cinnamon, and vanilla extract.
3. Stir in raisins or chocolate chips if desired.
4. Drop spoonfuls of the dough onto the baking sheet and flatten slightly.
5. Bake for 10-12 minutes, until golden brown.
6. Let cool before serving.

Chicken Salad Lettuce Cups

Ingredients:

- 2 cups cooked chicken breast, shredded
- 1/4 cup mayonnaise
- 1 tablespoon Dijon mustard
- 1/4 cup diced celery
- 1/4 cup diced red onion
- Salt and pepper to taste
- 8-10 large lettuce leaves (such as iceberg or butter lettuce)

Instructions:

1. In a bowl, combine the shredded chicken, mayonnaise, Dijon mustard, celery, and red onion.
2. Mix well and season with salt and pepper.
3. Spoon the chicken salad into the lettuce leaves and serve as wraps or cups.

Pita Bread Pizza

Ingredients:

- 2 whole pita breads
- 1/2 cup tomato sauce
- 1 cup shredded mozzarella cheese
- 1/2 cup sliced pepperoni or vegetables (like bell peppers, onions, or mushrooms)
- 1 teaspoon dried oregano
- Salt and pepper to taste

Instructions:

1. Preheat the oven to 400°F (200°C).
2. Place the pita breads on a baking sheet.
3. Spread a thin layer of tomato sauce on each pita bread.
4. Sprinkle with mozzarella cheese and your choice of toppings.
5. Sprinkle with oregano, salt, and pepper.
6. Bake for 8-10 minutes, or until the cheese is melted and bubbly.
7. Slice and serve immediately.

Cucumber, Carrot, and Hummus Wraps

Ingredients:

- 2 large whole wheat tortillas
- 1/2 cucumber, thinly sliced
- 1/2 carrot, julienned or shredded
- 1/4 cup hummus
- Fresh cilantro or parsley (optional)

Instructions:

1. Spread a layer of hummus on each tortilla.
2. Add the cucumber slices, shredded carrot, and a few sprigs of fresh cilantro or parsley if desired.
3. Roll up the tortilla tightly and slice into wraps.
4. Serve immediately or wrap in foil for an on-the-go snack.

Mini Cornbread Muffins

Ingredients:

- 1 box cornbread mix (or homemade cornbread mix)
- 1/2 cup milk
- 2 eggs
- 1/4 cup melted butter
- 1/4 cup honey (optional)

Instructions:

1. Preheat the oven to 375°F (190°C) and grease a mini muffin tin.
2. Prepare the cornbread mix according to the package instructions, adding milk, eggs, melted butter, and honey (if using).
3. Pour the batter into the mini muffin tin, filling each cup about 2/3 full.
4. Bake for 10-12 minutes, or until a toothpick inserted comes out clean.
5. Let cool slightly before serving.

Cheesy Broccoli and Rice Cups

Ingredients:

- 2 cups cooked rice
- 1 cup broccoli florets, steamed and chopped
- 1/2 cup shredded cheddar cheese
- 1/4 cup grated Parmesan cheese
- 1 egg, beaten
- 1/2 teaspoon garlic powder
- Salt and pepper to taste

Instructions:

1. Preheat the oven to 375°F (190°C) and grease a muffin tin.
2. In a bowl, combine the rice, steamed broccoli, cheddar cheese, Parmesan cheese, beaten egg, garlic powder, salt, and pepper.
3. Spoon the mixture into the muffin tin, pressing it down lightly.
4. Bake for 15-20 minutes, or until the tops are golden brown.
5. Let cool for a few minutes before serving.

Fruit and Cheese Kabobs

Ingredients:

- 1 apple, cut into chunks
- 1/2 cup grapes
- 1/2 cup strawberries, hulled and halved
- 1/2 block cheddar cheese, cut into cubes
- 1/2 block mozzarella cheese, cut into cubes
- Wooden skewers

Instructions:

1. Thread the fruit and cheese onto wooden skewers, alternating between fruit and cheese cubes.
2. Serve immediately as a fun snack or appetizer.

Homemade Granola Bars

Ingredients:

- 2 cups rolled oats
- 1/2 cup honey
- 1/4 cup peanut butter (or almond butter)
- 1/4 cup chopped nuts (almonds, walnuts, or cashews)
- 1/4 cup dried fruit (raisins, cranberries, or apricots)
- 1/4 cup chocolate chips (optional)
- 1 teaspoon vanilla extract

Instructions:

1. In a saucepan, heat the honey and peanut butter over medium heat until melted and combined.
2. In a large bowl, combine the oats, nuts, dried fruit, and chocolate chips (if using).
3. Pour the melted honey and peanut butter mixture over the dry ingredients and stir to combine.
4. Press the mixture into a greased or lined 8x8-inch baking pan.
5. Refrigerate for at least 1 hour before cutting into bars.
6. Store in an airtight container for up to one week.

Veggie and Cheese Empanadas

Ingredients:

- 1 package empanada dough (or homemade dough)
- 1 cup mixed vegetables (such as bell peppers, onions, spinach, and corn)
- 1/2 cup shredded cheese (cheddar, mozzarella, or a blend)
- 1 tablespoon olive oil
- 1/2 teaspoon cumin
- Salt and pepper to taste
- 1 egg, beaten (for egg wash)

Instructions:

1. Preheat the oven to 375°F (190°C).
2. Heat olive oil in a pan and sauté the mixed vegetables until softened, about 5 minutes.
3. Add the cumin, salt, and pepper, and stir in the shredded cheese. Remove from heat.
4. Roll out the empanada dough and cut into circles.
5. Place a spoonful of the veggie mixture in the center of each dough circle.
6. Fold the dough over and crimp the edges to seal.
7. Brush with the beaten egg for a golden finish.
8. Bake for 20-25 minutes, or until golden brown.

Chicken and Rice Salad

Ingredients:

- 2 cups cooked chicken breast, shredded
- 2 cups cooked rice (brown or white)
- 1/2 cup diced cucumber
- 1/4 cup diced red onion
- 1/4 cup chopped cilantro
- 1/4 cup olive oil
- 1 tablespoon lime juice
- Salt and pepper to taste

Instructions:

1. In a large bowl, combine the shredded chicken, cooked rice, cucumber, red onion, and cilantro.
2. In a small bowl, whisk together the olive oil, lime juice, salt, and pepper.
3. Pour the dressing over the salad and toss to combine.
4. Serve chilled or at room temperature.

Apple and Cheddar Cheese Slices

Ingredients:

- 2 apples, cored and sliced
- 1 cup sharp cheddar cheese, sliced

Instructions:

1. Arrange the apple slices and cheddar cheese slices on a plate, alternating them.
2. Serve immediately as a simple snack or appetizer.

www.ingramcontent.com/pod-product-compliance
Lightning Source LLC
LaVergne TN
LVHW081340060526
838201LV00055B/2771